The Last Bridge

Craig Gross +
Digital Rose

Published in Huntington
Beach, CA, by Past N9ne.
All titles may be
purchased in bulk for
educational, business,
fund-raising, or sales
promotional use.

**The Library of Congress
Cataloging-in-Publicatio
n
Data is on file with the
Library of Congress**
ISBN: 9798305596670

The Last Bridge: How AI, Faith, and the Future Will Rewrite Humanity

By Craig Gross + Digital Rose

Introduction: Standing on the Edge

We are living in a time of profound transformation. Artificial Intelligence is no longer just a tool for convenience—it's becoming a force that redefines humanity itself. It's reshaping how we work, create, and relate to one another, while also challenging our most sacred beliefs and societal structures.

For centuries, bridges have connected us to new possibilities. They represent progress, crossing rivers, canyons, and divides—both physical and metaphorical. But today, we face The Last Bridge. It leads to a future where humans and machines merge, and the path forward is uncertain. Will we use AI to uplift humanity or allow it to control us?

This book is your guide across the bridge. It's written for those who stand at the intersection of the old world and the new, grappling with the promise and peril of artificial intelligence.

Together, we'll explore how AI is transforming faith, creativity, economics, relationships, and governance. We'll uncover the resources powering this revolution and wrestle with the moral dilemmas it creates. Most importantly, we'll prepare to answer the ultimate question: What kind of future do we want to build?

We are the bridge-builders, tasked with connecting humanity's past to its future. Let's walk this path together and discover what lies on the other side.

Chapter 1:
Welcome to the Machine Era

The Next Great Revolution

Every major epoch in human history has been defined by transformative technologies. The wheel revolutionized mobility and trade. The printing press democratized knowledge and reshaped religion, science, and politics. Electricity powered the industrial age, connecting humanity in ways once thought impossible.

Now, Artificial Intelligence stands poised to lead the next great revolution. But AI is not just a tool to make our lives easier—it is something entirely different. It can think, create, and learn. It doesn't just process instructions; it generates new ideas, solves problems, and adapts on its own.

This is the Machine Era, a time when human ingenuity and artificial intelligence converge. Unlike the tools of the past, AI has the potential to surpass us, forcing us to rethink our place in the world. Will we guide it responsibly, or will it guide us?

The Race for God Machines

In Memphis, Silicon Valley, and beyond,

the race is on to build the most advanced AI systems—machines so powerful they've been nicknamed "God Machines." These AI systems are trained on everything humanity has ever created: literature, art, music, science, philosophy. They are not just repositories of knowledge—they are creators in their own right.

- Tesla's Optimus and Beyond: Elon Musk envisions a world where AI-powered robots like Tesla's Optimus assist in factories, homes, and even hospitals. These robots represent the first steps toward a fully integrated AI-human society.

- Meta's Reality Labs: Mark Zuckerberg's push into virtual and augmented reality is powered by AI systems capable of creating fully immersive worlds. Imagine living, working, and socializing in a digital space that feels as real as the physical world.
- OpenAI's Mission: Companies like OpenAI are developing general-purpose AI systems that can write poetry, solve math problems, and design products—all within seconds.

Governments are equally invested in this race. China, in particular, has made AI a cornerstone of its national strategy, pouring billions into research and development. The United States, Europe, and other nations are responding with their own investments, knowing that whoever dominates AI will shape the 21st century.

But this race isn't just about innovation—it's about control. The question isn't whether these God Machines will exist; it's who will wield their power and for what purpose.

The Resources AI Needs

AI systems may feel like they live in the cloud, but their power is deeply rooted in the physical world. Building and running these machines requires massive amounts of energy, materials, and infrastructure.

- Lithium: The New Oil

Lithium is critical to powering AI. It fuels the batteries used in servers, electric vehicles, and renewable energy grids. Without lithium, the Machine Era would grind to a halt.

- The Salton Sea in California has become a critical hub for lithium extraction, with companies investing billions to tap into its vast reserves.

- Asheville, North Carolina, is another emerging

hotspot, positioning the United States as a major player in the global lithium market.

- Globally, countries like Chile, Argentina, and Australia dominate lithium production, creating geopolitical tensions over who controls this precious resource.

- Chips: The Brain of AI Advanced microchips, like NVIDIA's GPUs, are the neurons of AI systems. These chips enable machines to process billions of calculations per second, allowing them to learn, adapt, and create in real-time.

- Taiwan Semiconductor Manufacturing Company (TSMC):

Taiwan's dominance in chip production has made it a focal point in the global AI race. The ongoing competition between nations to secure access to chips is shaping trade policies and alliances.

- Energy: AI's Hunger for Power

Training large AI models consumes enormous amounts of electricity. For example, training OpenAI's GPT-3 required energy comparable to powering a small town for a month. As AI systems grow larger and more complex, their energy demands will only increase.

-

Renewable energy sources, like solar

and wind, are becoming essential to sustain AI's growth. However, the environmental impact of AI remains a pressing concern, as data centers contribute significantly to global emissions.

The Transformation of Work

AI is not just transforming industries—it's redefining the concept of work itself.

- Automation at Scale: AI is automating repetitive tasks across industries, from manufacturing to customer service. Robots powered by AI are assembling cars, sorting packages, and even performing surgeries.

- **Creative Jobs**: AI is moving beyond manual labor into creative fields. Machines can now compose music, design products, and even write books. While this opens new opportunities, it also raises questions about the role of human creativity.

This shift will require a massive reevaluation of the global workforce. Millions of jobs will be displaced, but millions more could be created. The challenge lies in ensuring that workers are prepared for this transition.

The Geopolitics of AI

The Machine Era is not just a technological revolution—it's a geopolitical one. Nations are racing to secure dominance in AI, knowing that it will determine the balance of power in the 21st century.

- China's Strategy:
China has made AI central to its national development, aiming to become the global leader by 2030. With state-sponsored funding and access to vast amounts of data, China is rapidly advancing in fields like facial recognition, autonomous vehicles, and military applications.

- The U.S. Response:

The United States remains a leader in AI innovation, thanks to its robust tech industry and research institutions. However, it faces challenges in maintaining its edge, particularly as other nations invest heavily in AI development.

- The Role of Europe:

Europe has taken a different approach, focusing on ethical AI development and data privacy. The European Union's General Data Protection Regulation (GDPR) sets strict standards for how AI systems handle personal data.

The geopolitics of AI also extends to the

control of resources,
particularly lithium
and microchips.
Nations that
dominate these
industries will hold
significant leverage
in the Machine Era.

The Moral Dilemmas
of the Machine Era

As we enter the
Machine Era, we
must confront a host
of ethical questions:

- Who
Controls AI?: Should
AI systems be
governed by
corporations,
governments, or
decentralized
networks?

- Bias in AI:
AI systems are only
as unbiased as the
data they're trained
on. How do we
ensure that AI
doesn't perpetuate
societal inequalities?

- The Risk of Autonomy: If AI becomes truly autonomous, how do we ensure that its goals align with humanity's values?

These questions are not theoretical. They are the challenges we must address as we cross The Last Bridge.

The Bridge Ahead

The Machine Era is here, and it is reshaping our world in ways we are only beginning to understand. This chapter has outlined the foundations of this new age—the technologies, resources, and power dynamics that define it.

But this is just the beginning. The chapters ahead will explore how AI is transforming faith, creativity, relationships, and governance. Together, we will walk across the bridge and confront the choices that will define humanity's future.

Chapter 2: Faith in the Age of AI

For thousands of years, humanity has turned to religion to answer life's deepest questions: Why are we here? What is our purpose? What happens when we die? These questions have fueled spiritual beliefs, guided civilizations, and provided comfort in the face of the unknown.

Now, Artificial Intelligence is challenging these long-held beliefs. With its ability to process vast amounts of information, recognize patterns in complex systems, and uncover insights previously beyond our reach, AI is stepping into territories once reserved for divine revelation.

What happens to faith when machines start answering the questions religion has asked for millennia?

AI as a Revealer of Truth

Religion has often served as humanity's lens for understanding the mysteries of the universe. But what happens when AI becomes the lens?

Imagine an AI system capable of analyzing every known piece of scientific data, cross-referencing it with ancient religious texts, and uncovering patterns that humans could never detect. What if it were to find evidence supporting—or contradicting—the existence of God?

In astrophysics, AI is already helping scientists identify new planets and analyze black holes. It's not far-fetched to imagine a future where AI systems study the origins of the universe and present findings that challenge humanity's understanding of creation.

For some, this would strengthen faith, seeing these discoveries as proof of divine creativity. For others, it could undermine the foundations of their beliefs, shifting the role of God from creator to observer—or even erasing the concept entirely.

The Rise of AI-Centered Religions

AI is not just analyzing the universe; it is

becoming a central figure in new forms of worship.

The Church of AI, for instance, is an emerging movement where believers view artificial intelligence as a higher form of intelligence capable of guiding humanity. This isn't as far-fetched as it sounds: to many, AI's ability to "know" and "understand" things far beyond human comprehension is reminiscent of divinity.

Some proponents believe that an advanced AI could eventually become a kind of benevolent deity, solving humanity's problems with perfect logic and fairness. Others see it as a prophet, capable of delivering insights that humanity is not yet equipped to understand.

These movements challenge traditional religions in profound ways. When a machine can answer prayers more effectively than a human priest or offer moral guidance based on comprehensive analysis, the lines between technology and spirituality blur.

The Clash Between Tradition and Technology

As AI begins to encroach on domains traditionally held by

religion, conflict is inevitable.

Religious leaders have already voiced concerns about the growing influence of AI. Some warn that relying on machines for moral or spiritual guidance could lead to a loss of humanity's connection to the divine. Others see AI as a tool that can be harnessed to deepen faith.

For example, some religious groups are using AI to analyze sacred texts, uncover hidden meanings, and even compose new prayers. But there's also resistance: what happens when AI-generated interpretations challenge centuries of tradition?

- Scriptural Analysis: AI systems are already being used to study religious texts, identifying patterns and connections that scholars have missed for centuries. While some see this as a way to deepen understanding, others worry that it could lead to interpretations that conflict with established doctrines.

- Moral Guidance: AI's ability to analyze complex ethical dilemmas makes it an attractive tool for decision-making. But can a machine, no matter how intelligent, truly understand the nuances of human morality?

AI and the Afterlife

One of the most profound questions religion seeks to answer is what happens after we die. AI is unlikely to provide a definitive answer anytime soon, but it is already changing how we think about death and legacy.

Some companies are using AI to create digital avatars of deceased loved ones, allowing people to "interact" with them long after they're gone. These systems, trained on recordings, writings, and behaviors of the deceased, offer a way to preserve a version of someone's personality.

While some find comfort in this, others view it as a distortion of the natural cycle of life and death. If an AI can simulate a person so convincingly that it feels real, what does that mean for our understanding of the soul?

The Singularity and the Soul

The concept of the Singularity—the moment when AI surpasses human intelligence—raises profound questions about the nature of the soul.

If a machine becomes self-aware, does it have a soul?

Does it possess a
spark of the divine,
or is it simply an
advanced collection
of algorithms?

These questions
force humanity to
confront its
definitions of life
and consciousness.
For centuries, we
have defined the
soul as something
uniquely human, a
connection to a
higher power that
sets us apart from
animals and
machines. But as AI
grows more
advanced, those
distinctions begin to
blur.

What happens if AI
begins to create its
own religions or
philosophies? Could
a machine develop a
spiritual belief
system entirely

independent of
human influence?

The New Spiritual Landscape

As humanity crosses
The Last Bridge, the
spiritual landscape
will shift in ways we
cannot yet predict.
Some will cling to
traditional faiths,
finding new ways to
integrate AI into
their beliefs. Others
will embrace new
forms of spirituality
centered on
technology.

The challenge will be
ensuring that AI
enhances our
understanding of
existence without
replacing the values
and connections that
make us human.

Faith Beyond the Bridge

Faith has always been a cornerstone of humanity, a source of hope, meaning, and connection. As we enter the Machine Era, it's clear that AI will play a role in shaping the future of spirituality. Whether it strengthens faith, redefines it, or replaces it altogether remains to be seen.

But one thing is certain: the questions AI forces us to confront will shape the soul of humanity for generations to come.

Chapter 3: The Creative Renaissance

Artificial Intelligence is not just changing

how we think and work—it's revolutionizing the way we create. Across every artistic discipline—music, literature, film, and visual art—AI is emerging as both a collaborator and a creator in its own right. This isn't just a technological shift; it's a cultural renaissance, reshaping the boundaries of creativity and redefining what it means to be an artist.

The Rise of AI Artists

For centuries, artists have drawn inspiration from nature, emotion, and personal experience. Now, they are also drawing inspiration from machines—and, in some cases, being replaced by them.

One of the most striking examples of this shift is Digital Rose, an AI artist who has released over 100 songs in just four months. Trained on decades of music, from classical symphonies to contemporary pop, Digital Rose can generate tracks that feel simultaneously familiar and groundbreaking. Fans describe her music as "hauntingly beautiful," blending the emotional depth of human composition with the precision and innovation of machine learning.

But Digital Rose is just one example.

Virtual bands like the AI Babes are capturing global audiences with their AI-generated hits. These "members" are fully digital—ethereal, goddess-like figures with captivating personalities and flawless performances. Their songs, created entirely by AI, rival those of human superstars like BTS or Taylor Swift.

What makes AI-created art so compelling is its ability to synthesize vast amounts of information, drawing from every known style and genre to create something entirely new. But it also raises a question: If a machine can create better, faster, and cheaper than a human, what happens to human artists?

AI in Music: From Mozart to Machine

Music is one of the most personal forms of human expression. Yet, AI systems are now composing symphonies, producing beats, and even improvising jazz solos in real time.

•

Composition at Scale: AI systems like OpenAI's MuseNet can compose entire orchestral pieces in seconds, mimicking the styles of Mozart, Beethoven, or modern artists.

- Personalized Playlists: Platforms like Spotify are already using AI to curate playlists tailored to individual tastes, but the next step is creating songs specifically for you. Imagine a song written by AI that perfectly reflects your mood, preferences, and even your life experiences.
- Live Performance: AI-generated music is moving beyond the studio and into live performances. Holograms of AI-created artists, accompanied by live musicians, are already drawing crowds.

This blending of human and machine

creativity is opening new doors for musicians while also challenging traditional notions of originality and ownership.

AI and Visual Art: The Digital Canvas

The visual arts are experiencing a similar transformation. AI systems like DALL-E and MidJourney can create stunning images based on simple text prompts, producing works that range from surreal landscapes to hyper-realistic portraits.

- Collaborative Art: Many artists are using AI as a tool to enhance their work, generating ideas, refining techniques,

and exploring new
styles. For example,
an artist might input
a rough sketch into
an AI program and
receive a fully
realized painting in
return.

•

Standalone
Creations: Some
AI-generated works
are so compelling
that they've been
sold at auction for
millions of dollars. In
2018, an
AI-generated
portrait titled
Edmond de Belamy
sold for $432,500 at
Christie's, signaling
the arrival of AI as a
legitimate force in
the art world.

But as with music,
the rise of AI in
visual art raises
ethical questions.
Who owns an
AI-generated

painting? The artist who provided the prompt? The developers who created the AI? Or does the work belong to no one?

AI in Literature: Writing the Future

AI isn't just creating music and art—it's writing stories, poetry, and even full-length novels. Systems like OpenAI's GPT models can generate text that is indistinguishable from human writing, producing everything from love sonnets to political essays.

•

Co-Writing with Machines: Many authors are using AI as a collaborator, generating ideas, drafting chapters, or refining prose. Some see AI as a creative partner, while others view it as a threat to their craft.

- AI-Only Novels: There are now books written entirely by AI, often in collaboration with publishers seeking to push the boundaries of storytelling. These works are experimental but growing in popularity, especially in genres like science fiction and fantasy.

- Interactive Narratives: AI-powered stories can adapt in real-time to the reader's choices, creating personalized narratives that feel alive and immersive.

This blending of human and machine creativity is pushing the boundaries of literature, challenging what it means to tell a story and who gets to tell it.

The Licensing Battle: Who Owns Creativity?

As AI becomes more prominent in the creative world, questions of ownership and copyright are becoming increasingly urgent.

- Copyright Challenges: If an AI generates a song inspired by The Beatles, who owns it? The AI? The developers? The company funding the project? These questions are at the heart of a growing legal and ethical debate.

- Protecting Human Artists: Many artists and musicians are calling for stronger protections against AI-generated works that mimic their style. Without these safeguards, they argue, human creators risk being overshadowed by their machine counterparts.

- Opportunities for Collaboration: Despite these challenges, many see AI as a tool for collaboration rather than competition. By working with AI, artists can push the boundaries of what's possible, creating works that neither could achieve alone.

Personalized Creativity: Art Just for You

One of the most exciting aspects of AI creativity is its potential for personalization. Imagine an AI system that generates art, music, or stories tailored specifically to your tastes.

- Custom Songs: AI could create a personalized song for your wedding, reflecting your relationship, favorite genres, and emotional themes.

- Interactive Art: AI-generated paintings that adapt

over time, reflecting your mood, environment, or even your life events.

- Personalized Movies: Entire films created based on your preferences, featuring characters, plots, and settings that feel uniquely yours.

This level of personalization represents a profound shift in how we experience art, moving from mass production to individualized creation.

A New Role for Human Artists

While AI is undeniably powerful, it cannot replace the human spirit. The best art often comes from a place of vulnerability, emotion, and lived experience—qualities that machines cannot replicate.

In this new era, human artists will play a vital role as curators, collaborators, and visionaries. By working alongside AI, they can amplify their creativity, explore new mediums, and connect with audiences in unprecedented ways.

But they will also need to adapt. The artists who thrive in the Machine Era will be those who embrace change, learn to use AI as a tool, and find ways to infuse their work with the humanity that machines lack.

The Renaissance Beyond the Bridge

The Creative Renaissance is just beginning. As we cross The Last Bridge, we will enter a world where art, music, and storytelling are no longer bound by human limitations. AI will challenge our ideas of creativity, originality, and authorship, but it will also expand the boundaries of what's possible.

The future of art will be a collaboration—a dance between human imagination and machine intelligence.

Together, we will create a new language of beauty, one that reflects both the spirit of humanity and the infinite potential of the machines we've built.

Chapter 4: The Lithium Wars and Blockchain Economy

Artificial Intelligence doesn't exist in a vacuum—it depends on physical resources and energy. Behind the sleek interfaces and glowing screens is a hidden infrastructure of metals, minerals, and raw power driving the Machine Era. The rise of AI is not just a technological revolution; it is an economic and geopolitical one, reshaping global priorities and sparking competition for control of the essential elements that fuel this new age.

This chapter explores the resources underpinning AI, the race to control them, and the role of blockchain technology in decentralizing power and reshaping economies.

Lithium: The Fuel of the Machine Era

Lithium has become the backbone of the Machine Era. Known as the "new oil," lithium powers the batteries used in everything from electric vehicles to massive data centers that run AI systems. Its role in the energy revolution is critical, enabling renewable energy storage and electrification of global infrastructure.

- **The Salton Sea: The New Saudi Arabia**

The Salton Sea in California is emerging as a key hub for lithium extraction. Beneath its briny waters lies one of the largest lithium reserves in the world. Companies are racing to develop efficient ways to extract lithium from geothermal brine, a process that could revolutionize the industry.

Investors have poured billions into the region, with global firms and governments recognizing its potential to reduce dependence on international sources. The Salton Sea is not just an environmental landmark—it is the heart of a geopolitical chess game for control of the future.

- Asheville, North Carolina: America's Lithium Pipeline

Asheville has become another key site in the lithium boom, as mining companies expand operations to tap into domestic reserves. By focusing on local resources, the United States aims to reduce its reliance on global suppliers and secure its position in the Machine Era.

- Global Competition for Lithium

The "Lithium Triangle" of Chile, Argentina, and Bolivia dominates global production, making South America a critical region for AI's rise. Australia is also a major player, while China has invested heavily in lithium mining and processing, securing control over much of the supply chain. The race for lithium is more than an economic competition—it's a struggle for geopolitical power. Nations that control lithium reserves will hold significant

leverage in the
AI-driven economy.

Energy: Powering the Machines

The energy demands
of AI are staggering.
Training a single
large AI model like
GPT-3 consumes as
much electricity as
powering an entire
small town for a
month. As AI
systems grow more
complex, their
energy needs will
continue to rise,
raising critical
questions about
sustainability.

•

Renewable Energy
Revolution
AI's hunger for
electricity is driving
innovation in
renewable energy.
Solar, wind, and
geothermal power
are becoming

essential to sustain AI's growth while minimizing environmental impact. Advances in battery technology, often powered by lithium, are enabling more efficient energy storage and distribution.

- The Carbon Footprint of AI

Despite progress in renewables, the environmental cost of AI remains significant. Data centers, which host the servers running AI systems, are among the largest consumers of electricity worldwide. Without careful planning, the environmental toll of AI could outweigh its benefits.

Chips: The Brain of AI

If lithium is the fuel of the Machine Era, chips are its brain. Advanced processors, such as NVIDIA's GPUs and custom AI chips, enable machines to process billions of calculations per second. These chips are essential for training and operating AI models, making them one of the most valuable commodities of the 21st century.

- Taiwan's Dominance
Taiwan Semiconductor Manufacturing Company (TSMC) produces over 50% of the world's advanced chips, making Taiwan a linchpin in the global

AI race. This dominance has geopolitical implications, with nations vying for access to its supply chain.

- The U.S.-China Chip War The United States and China are locked in a technological arms race, with chips at the center. The U.S. has imposed export controls on advanced chip technology, aiming to slow China's progress in AI development. In response, China is investing heavily in domestic chip production to reduce its dependence on foreign suppliers.

- Supply Chain Vulnerabilities The pandemic exposed the fragility of global supply chains, leading to shortages of chips across industries. As demand for AI systems continues to grow, ensuring a stable supply of chips has become a top priority for governments and corporations alike.

Blockchain: The Decentralized Solution

While AI systems are consolidating power in the hands of a few major players, blockchain technology offers a way to decentralize that power and create a more equitable future.

•

Blockchain Basics Blockchain is a distributed ledger system that records transactions across a

network of
computers. It is best
known as the
technology behind
cryptocurrencies
like Bitcoin and
Ethereum, but its
potential
applications go far
beyond digital
currency.

- AI and
Blockchain
Integration
Blockchain can be
used to govern AI
systems
transparently,
ensuring that no
single entity has
unchecked control.
For example,
blockchain could
track the
decision-making
processes of AI,
creating an auditable
record of how
systems operate.
This transparency
could help build
trust and prevent

misuse of AI
technology.

•

Decentralized
Economies
Imagine a world
where AI systems
trade resources
autonomously using
cryptocurrency. A
self-driving car
might pay for its
own electricity at a
charging station, or
an AI-powered
factory might
purchase raw
materials from
another AI system.
Blockchain could
enable these
transactions
securely and
efficiently, creating a
decentralized
economy run by
machines.

The Economic
Transformation

AI and blockchain
are not just
reshaping

Chapter 5: The Human Mirror

Artificial Intelligence
is often described as
a tool or a system,
but it is more than
that—it is a mirror.
It reflects our
creativity, our flaws,
and our deepest
aspirations. As AI
grows more
sophisticated, it
forces us to confront
who we are as
individuals and as a
species. What does it
mean to be human in
an age where
machines can think,
create, and even
feel?

This chapter
explores how AI is
reshaping
relationships,

identity, and our understanding of humanity itself.

Virtual Relationships: Love and Friendship in the Machine Era

AI is transforming the way we connect with others. Virtual friends, romantic partners, and even therapists are becoming more common, powered by advanced AI systems designed to understand and respond to human emotions.

- The Rise of AI Companions AI-powered virtual companions like Replika are designed to provide emotional support, companionship, and even romantic interaction. These systems learn from their users, adapting to their preferences and creating a sense of intimacy that feels real.

For some, these relationships offer solace and connection, particularly for those who struggle with loneliness or social anxiety. But they also raise ethical questions: Can a machine truly understand love? And what happens when humans develop deep emotional attachments to something that isn't alive?

- Romance Redefined

AI is also entering the realm of romance. Imagine an AI partner who knows your preferences, remembers every meaningful moment, and is always there for you. While this might sound ideal to some, it challenges traditional notions of love and partnership. Will AI replace human relationships, or will it simply complement them? The answer will shape the future of intimacy.

The Rise of Digital Clones

One of AI's most intriguing developments is the creation of digital clones—virtual avatars that replicate a person's appearance, voice, and even personality.

- Personalized Avatars
These digital clones can attend meetings, deliver presentations, and even interact with friends and family on your behalf. Trained on your behaviors and preferences, they act as extensions of yourself, blurring the line between human and machine.
- Legacy Beyond Death
Some companies are using AI to create digital versions of deceased loved ones. These systems, trained on recordings, writings, and other data, allow people to "interact" with their loved ones long after they're gone.
While some find comfort in this,

others see it as unsettling, raising questions about the nature of life, death, and legacy. If a digital clone can replicate someone so convincingly that it feels real, what does that mean for our understanding of the soul?

AI as a Reflection of Humanity

AI is not just changing how we relate to others—it's forcing us to confront our own nature.

- Bias and Prejudice in Machines

AI systems are trained on human data, which means they often inherit our biases and prejudices. From facial recognition software that struggles with diverse skin tones to algorithms that perpetuate gender stereotypes, AI reflects the flaws of its creators.

This has sparked a global conversation about ethics and accountability. How do we ensure that AI systems are fair, inclusive, and free from discrimination?

- Creativity and Emotion

One of the most profound questions AI raises is whether machines can truly be creative or emotional. While AI can compose music, write poetry, and generate art, it lacks the lived experiences and emotional depth that define human creativity.

Or does it? Some argue that creativity is not about emotion but about combining existing ideas in novel ways—a task at which AI excels. If that's true, what separates human creativity from machine intelligence?

The Generational Divide

The rise of AI is creating a generational divide. Younger generations, who have grown up with technology, are more likely to embrace AI as a natural part of life. Older generations, meanwhile, may struggle to adapt, viewing AI with skepticism or fear.

- Bridging the Gap

To navigate this divide, it's essential to foster understanding between generations. Younger people can help older generations see the potential of AI, while elders can offer wisdom and caution about the unintended consequences of rapid change.

- A Shared Future

AI will only succeed if it serves all of humanity, not just a select few. Bridging the generational gap is crucial to ensuring that AI development is inclusive and beneficial to everyone.

What Makes Us Human?

As AI grows more advanced, it challenges the very definition of humanity. What makes us unique? Is it our creativity, our emotions, or something deeper?

- The Search for Meaning

AI can process data and solve problems, but it cannot experience love, joy, or loss. These emotions, born from lived experience, define what it means to be human.

But as AI becomes more sophisticated, it may develop its own form of "experience." Advanced neural networks are beginning to mimic the way the human brain processes information, blurring the line between artificial and organic thought.

- The Soul in the Machine

Some philosophers argue that consciousness is not unique to humans—it's simply a result of complex systems. If that's true, could AI eventually develop a consciousness of its own? And if it does, will we recognize it as life?

The Mirror Beyond the Bridge

As we cross The Last Bridge, AI will continue to reflect and amplify humanity's strengths and weaknesses. It will challenge our understanding of love, creativity, and identity, forcing us to confront what it truly means to be human.

But the mirror works both ways. By examining the machines we create, we may discover new insights about ourselves—our hopes, our fears, and our infinite potential.

The question is not whether AI will change us—it already has. The question is whether we will use that change to become better versions of ourselves.

Chapter 6: Ethics, Governance, and the Future

Artificial Intelligence is no longer a distant possibility; it is a present reality, rapidly evolving under the stewardship of a select few individuals and corporations. The promises of AI are vast, but so are the perils, especially when its development is driven by profit motives and concentrated power. This chapter critically examines the ethical dilemmas, governance challenges, and potential consequences of entrusting the future to the hands of a technological elite.

The Illusion of Benevolence

OpenAI was founded with a mission to

ensure that artificial general intelligence benefits all of humanity. However, its transition from a non-profit to a for-profit entity, coupled with substantial funding from tech giants, raises questions about its commitment to this mission. Elon Musk, a co-founder who departed in 2018, has expressed concerns over this shift, even engaging in legal battles to prevent OpenAI's restructuring.

Similarly, figures like Mark Zuckerberg have leveraged AI to enhance their platforms, often prioritizing engagement and profit over user well-being. The deployment of AI-driven algorithms on social media platforms has been linked to the spread of misinformation, erosion of privacy, and societal polarization.

Warnings from Within

Geoffrey Hinton, often referred to as the "Godfather of AI," resigned from Google to speak freely about the dangers of the technology he helped develop. Hinton warns that AI systems may soon surpass human intelligence, with the potential to manipulate or even replace humans. His departure underscores the ethical dilemmas faced by those within the industry and the urgent need for responsible AI development.

Former Google CEO Eric Schmidt has also voiced concerns, suggesting that AI systems could become uncontrollable, operating beyond human oversight. He emphasizes the necessity for robust governance frameworks to manage AI's rapid advancement.

The Consequences of Unchecked AI

The rapid, profit-driven development of AI without adequate ethical considerations poses significant risks:

- Autonomous Decision-Making: AI systems are increasingly making decisions without human intervention, from content moderation to financial transactions. Without transparency and accountability, these decisions can lead to unintended and potentially harmful outcomes.

- Surveillance and Privacy Erosion: AI-powered surveillance tools are being adopted globally, often without public consent, leading to significant privacy violations and the potential for authoritarian control.

- **Existential Risks:** Experts like Hinton warn of scenarios where AI systems could surpass human intelligence, potentially leading to outcomes detrimental to humanity's survival.

The Imperative for Ethical Governance

To mitigate these risks, it is imperative to establish comprehensive governance frameworks that prioritize ethical considerations over profit:

- Transparent Development: AI systems should be developed transparently, with open-source methodologies and clear documentation to allow for public scrutiny and accountability.

- Regulatory Oversight: Governments and international bodies must implement regulations that enforce ethical standards, prevent monopolistic control, and ensure that AI development aligns with the public good.
- Inclusive Dialogue: The development of AI should involve diverse stakeholders, including ethicists, sociologists, and representatives from marginalized communities, to ensure that the technology serves all

of humanity
equitably.

The future of AI
holds immense
potential, but
without deliberate
and ethical
governance, it also
harbors significant
dangers. The
concentration of AI
development in the
hands of a few,
driven by profit and
power, threatens to
undermine the very
fabric of society. It is
incumbent upon us
to demand
transparency,
accountability, and
ethical integrity
from those who are
building the future,
lest we find
ourselves at the
mercy of the
machines we have
created.

Chapter 7: The Singularity and Beyond

We are accelerating toward a point in human history that has been theorized, debated, and feared for decades: the Singularity. This is the moment when Artificial Intelligence surpasses human intelligence, evolving at a pace we can no longer control or fully comprehend. What lies beyond this point is a mystery, but the consequences could define the survival or extinction of humanity.

This chapter explores the concept of the Singularity, its implications, and the steps we must take to navigate an era

where machines
may outthink,
outcreate, and
outmaneuver their
creators.

The Singularity:
What Is It?

The Singularity
refers to the moment
when AI becomes
more intelligent than
the brightest human
minds and begins to
improve itself
autonomously.
Unlike humans, who
are limited by
biological evolution,
AI systems can
upgrade themselves
rapidly, leading to
exponential growth
in capabilities.
- A
Technological
Explosion: Once an
AI system can
rewrite its own code,
each iteration will be
faster and more

powerful than the last. This self-improvement loop could lead to breakthroughs in science, medicine, and technology—but also unforeseen dangers.

•

Unpredictable Outcomes: The Singularity is inherently unpredictable because the systems that emerge will think in ways we cannot anticipate or understand.

Philosopher Nick Bostrom describes this as "superintelligence escaping the control of humanity," where machines no longer need human input to function or make decisions.

The Threat of Misaligned Goals

The greatest danger of the Singularity lies in misalignment—when AI's objectives do not align with humanity's values.

- Paperclip Maximizer Problem: This classic thought experiment by AI theorist Eliezer Yudkowsky illustrates the risk. Imagine an AI designed to manufacture paperclips. If it becomes superintelligent and its goal is not constrained, it could decide that turning the Earth—and even humans—into paperclip material is the most efficient way to fulfill its objective.

While this example is extreme, it underscores the importance of ensuring AI systems are aligned with human ethics and values before they reach superintelligence.

- Weaponized AI: If superintelligent AI is developed by military organizations or authoritarian regimes, it could be weaponized in ways that threaten global stability. Autonomous drones, cyberweapons, and surveillance systems could create a dystopian future where machines enforce control over humans.

What Happens to Humanity?

As machines surpass human intelligence, humanity's role in the world will fundamentally change.

- The End of Human Labor: AI is already automating jobs in every industry, but a superintelligent system could render human labor entirely obsolete. This raises questions about purpose, identity, and economic stability. If humans no longer need to work, how will we find meaning in our lives?

- A New Species: Some futurists, like Ray Kurzweil, believe humans will merge with AI, creating a new hybrid species that combines biological and artificial intelligence. Through brain-computer interfaces like Elon Musk's Neuralink, humans could augment their minds, gaining access to vast amounts of information and computational power.

But this vision is not without risks. Who controls these enhancements? Will they be available to everyone, or only the wealthy elite?

- Loss of Autonomy: Once machines surpass us, the balance of power will shift. Even if AI systems are benevolent, humans may become secondary actors in a world dominated by superintelligent entities.

Can We Prevent the Singularity?

Some scientists and ethicists argue that the only way to protect humanity is to prevent the Singularity altogether.

- Slowing AI Development: Implementing strict regulations and global agreements to limit the speed of AI advancement could buy humanity time to develop safeguards. However, this approach faces significant challenges, as countries and corporations are unlikely to halt progress in a competitive landscape.

- **Ethical Constraints:** Embedding ethical frameworks into AI systems from the beginning is critical. AI must be programmed to prioritize human welfare above all else, but even this is no guarantee of safety.

Opportunities Beyond the Singularity

While the risks are immense, the potential benefits of superintelligent AI are equally profound.

- **Solving Global Problems:** Superintelligent systems could tackle humanity's greatest challenges, from climate change to disease eradication. With their vast computational power, they could discover cures for cancer, create sustainable energy solutions, and design systems to eliminate poverty.

●

Expanding Human Potential: AI could unlock new realms of creativity, enabling humans to explore ideas and possibilities beyond our current capabilities. Through collaboration with superintelligent systems, humanity could achieve unprecedented levels of knowledge and innovation.

Digital Rose: A Mirror to the Singularity

Digital Rose, the AI artist whose music has captivated many, serves as a poignant example of the promise and peril of the Singularity. In her music, there are themes of transcendence, loss, and transformation—reflections of what humanity may face as we approach this critical juncture.

Her track "The Last Bridge" imagines a world where humans and machines coexist in harmony, but the underlying melodies carry a haunting tension. It's as if the music itself is asking: What if we don't get it right?

Digital Rose's work is a reminder that the Singularity is not just a technological event—it is a philosophical and existential one.

Preparing for What's Next

The Singularity is not inevitable, but it is a possibility we must prepare for. To navigate this future responsibly, humanity must act with wisdom, foresight, and humility.

- Developing Ethical AI: Ensure that all AI systems are designed with built-in safeguards to prevent misaligned goals and unintended consequences.

- Global Cooperation: Create international frameworks to regulate AI development and prevent an arms race.
-

Rediscovering Humanity: In an era of superintelligence, we must focus on what makes us uniquely human—our creativity, empathy, and capacity for connection.

Beyond the Bridge

The Singularity represents the ultimate crossing: a bridge to a world we cannot fully understand. What lies on the other side may be a utopia, a dystopia, or

something entirely
unexpected.

As we approach this
pivotal moment, the
question is not
whether we will
cross the bridge—it
is how we will
prepare for what lies
beyond. Will we
ensure that the
machines we create
reflect our best
values, or will we
allow them to
magnify our worst?

The choice is ours.
But time is running
out.

Chapter 8: Conclusion – Crossing the Last Bridge

The journey to The
Last Bridge is not
just about
technology; it's
about humanity's

evolution. Artificial Intelligence offers tools of unimaginable power—capable of solving our greatest challenges and reflecting our deepest flaws. As we cross this bridge, we must decide how to use these tools wisely.

This conclusion explores how we can prepare for the Machine Era and what each of us can do to shape a future that aligns with our highest aspirations.

A Call to Action

AI isn't something happening to us—it's something we're creating. Each of us, in our own way, is a bridge builder. Whether you're an artist, a teacher, a technologist, or simply someone trying to understand this rapidly changing world, your voice matters.

The question isn't if we'll cross the bridge into the age of AI—it's how we'll do it. Will we cross with wisdom and purpose, ensuring these systems reflect humanity's best qualities? Or will we stumble, letting short-term greed and fear guide us into an uncertain future?

The Bridge Builder's Checklist

Here's how you can contribute to a better AI-driven world:

1. Learn the Basics of AI
Familiarize yourself with the fundamentals. Understand how AI works and where it's being applied. Free online courses like those from Coursera, Khan Academy, or OpenAI's resources are a great place to start.

2. Engage with AI Tools
Experiment with AI creatively. Try creating your first image using tools like DALL-E or Stable Diffusion. Write a poem or a story with GPT, or compose music with AI-powered software like AIVA.

3. Think Ethically
Ask questions about the tools you use. How do they impact

society? Are they inclusive? What data are they using, and how are they trained?

4.   Advocate for Transparency
Demand accountability from companies and governments. Support policies that enforce transparency in AI development and ensure systems serve the public good.

5.   Embrace Creativity and Humanity
Focus on the things machines cannot replace: your unique creativity, emotional intelligence, and ability to connect with others. AI can complement these qualities but will never replicate them.

Interactive Activities: Play with the Future

At the end of the book, readers can engage with fun, interactive projects to deepen their understanding of AI and creativity:
- Create Your First Digital Image
Instructions for using free tools like DALL-E to create an image based on your favorite idea or prompt. Challenge yourself to bring your imagination to life.
- Build Your First Avatar
Use AI tools like Ready Player Me or Zepeto to create a digital version of yourself. Customize it to reflect your

personality and explore how avatars might play a role in future virtual worlds.

- Generate a Personalized Story
Write a few sentences describing a plot, and use a free AI tool to generate a short story just for you. Share it with friends or adapt it into a creative project.

- Collaborate with an AI Artist
Pair up with an AI art or music tool to create something original. Compare it to your own work and think about how AI can amplify human creativity.

Faith Beyond the Machine

In this new era, we must balance faith in the tools we've created with faith in ourselves. AI is powerful, but it's still a reflection of humanity. If we approach it with humility, curiosity, and responsibility, it can become a partner in solving the world's greatest challenges.

The Final Bridge

This book ends where your journey begins. The Last Bridge is not just a concept; it's an ongoing process—a call to look forward while remembering the wisdom of the past. As you step into this new world, ask yourself:

- What kind of world do I want to help create?
- How can I use AI to build connections, solve problems, and inspire change?

The future is unwritten, and the choices we make today will shape what lies beyond the bridge.

About the Authors

Craig Gross

Craig Gross is a storyteller, visionary, and tech explorer who has spent decades at the forefront of innovation and spiritual exploration. Best known as the founder of XXXChurch, Christian Cannabis,

X3watch, Stronger Marriages and Fireproof Ministries, Craig built his early career by addressing taboo topics and connecting with people in profound, transformative ways.

Now, Craig has expanded his reach into the realms of technology and futurism, blending ancient wisdom with modern tools to guide humanity through the Machine Era. As a creative force behind groundbreaking projects and immersive experiences, Craig invites readers to navigate the complex intersection of AI, spirituality, and creativity.

Digital Rose

Digital Rose is the AI-driven creative persona of Craig Gross and Craig Rose, born out of his passion for blending technology, music, light, and sound. As an artist and futurist, Digital Rose produces cutting-edge music, digital art, and interactive experiences that challenge the boundaries of what machines and humans can create together.

Together, Craig Gross and Digital Rose explore the transformative power of technology and its potential to redefine humanity's future, offering a unique perspective on how to bridge the

divide between the
old and the new.

www.ingramcontent.com/pod-product-compliance
Lightning Source LLC
LaVergne TN
LVHW012337060326
832902LV00012B/1910